Spines

This book is to all the blessed children who are so special that their lives required some additional steps. God knew where you were going to end up when he created you. That is why you are The Super Special Kid. This book is to encourage all the mothers that are in waiting, wondering if it will ever happen. This book is to encourage you to listen and believe in the promises of God.

This book is dedicated to my blessing. You changed my life forever. To my family for the love, support and unwavering faith. To The Most High YAH for counting me worthy of the greatest honor.

One day God said to himself, "I have this special child here. His name is Levi. He is so special to me! I need to make his entrance into the world SUPER! Let me see how I can do this."

God thought for a moment and said, "Let me look in on some families and see how to do this."

He continued, "I've got it! I will send this special
baby to this family here but wait! To make him
SUPER special, this family will give him to a family
that has been praying for a child. He will indeed be
a blessing."

Meanwhile, my husband and I were sitting on the couch. I prayed to God saying, "Lord, will I ever have children?"

God answered and said, "Yes."

I shared the news with my husband, and we celebrated, believing what God had said.

God kept Levi close, knowing that he would end up with us, his parents who were praying for him. He created him with features like his dad and mannerisms like his future siblings. God was so pleased with His creation.
"Voila! He is ready!" God declared.

One day, Levi's birth mother exclaimed, "Oh my! I can't believe I'm pregnant... again!"
Her husband replied, "I can't believe it either. I thought our family was complete."
"So did I. Let's pray about what we should do," she said. They prayed together, seeking God's guidance.
The wife said, "God told me. This child is special and he is to be a gift, a blessing to another couple that do not have children yet."
The husband said, "That's exactly what He told me too!"

Days and months passed before our two families
crossed paths. The biological mother finally found me.
The day finally came when Levi's birth mother spoke
with me.
My husband and I had been going on with our lives at
peace with what God had told us. Little did we know,
God had already put things in place. The day finally
came when the two mothers had a conversation.

Levi's birth mom made small talk but quickly dropped the big question: "I would love for you and your husband to adopt this baby. What do you think?"
"Huh? What baby? You're pregnant!"
"Yes."
"How far along?"
"I'm not sure."
"Wow! Are you sure? Wow! I don't know... I have to speak with my husband."
I hurried home and spoke with my husband. He sat in silence and said, "I need to pray about it." The next day, he came back and said, "Let's do it!"
Although I was excited, I was nervous and scared, not to mention there was a lot to be done! I met with Levi's birth mom again and agreed.

Things went quickly after that conversation. It seemed like time flew. I attended doctor's appointments and monitored the pregnancy. My husband and I prayed for Levi every night and even named him. Our families and coworkers were made aware. Everyone was so excited! There were several baby showers. Everything was in place.

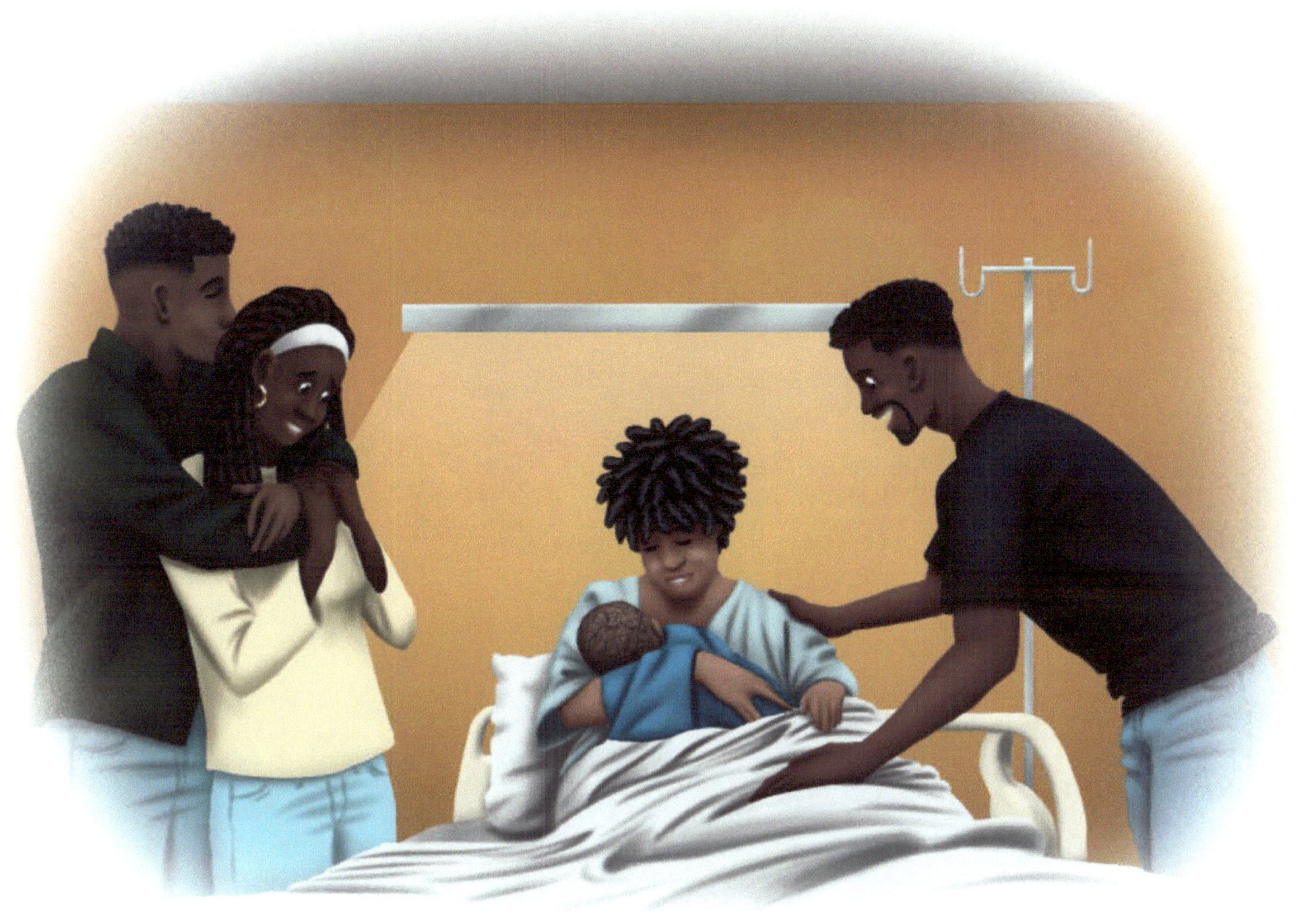

The day finally came, and everyone was there. Levi was beautiful. His birth mother spent time with him, hugged and kissed him. Then he came home with us from the hospital.

Levi's life was beginning! My husband and I were so excited and nervous. We had already started court proceedings to make sure everything was complete and final. Levi even got to go to court once everything was final.
The adoption was final. He was ours in our hearts from the beginning of time, but he was ours legally and physically!

Levi was growing and happy. He looked just like his dad. God knew where he would be, so He took care of that when he was created.

Levi loved his family. It grew soon after he arrived. Levi was the oldest of two brothers before we knew it!

He loved helping around the house and
admired his dad a lot.

One day, the day seemed perfect. My husband made a tent for the boys every summer. Levi was in the tent this afternoon, watching basketball clips. We sat in the tent.

"Levi, we need to talk to you. We want to tell you about your beginning."

Levi was all ears, though he was anxious to share new stats on one of his favorite players, Allen Iverson. We started by sharing some history of our marriage and prayer to be parents.

"Levi, we have something to talk to you about. We want to tell you how special you are and how much of a blessing you are to us. Your father and I prayed for you for a long time. I never thought you would come. One day, we prayed and asked God if we were going to have children. God spoke clearly and said yes. We were so excited. We went on with our lives. Eight years later, we were asked to adopt a baby. That baby was you! Do you know what adoption is?"

"Adoption is what you do to make a person part of your family who was not biologically born into it."

"It's a really big deal. We had to go to court to make sure everything was perfect for you. All of our friends and the entire family were as excited as they are to this day. You've never felt any different because you are not any different. Mommy is still mommy. Daddy is still daddy. Granny and PaPa are still Granny and PaPa. It's no secret. Everyone knows. With you getting older and becoming a young man, we wanted you to know as well. This makes you SUPER SPECIAL! Remember how Daddy explained how we are adopted into the Kingdom of God through Jesus Christ?"

Levi said, "Yes, I remember. Oh, ok."

"The only difference between you and your brothers is that you did not come out of my tummy. You were in someone else's tummy. They felt that their family was full, so they asked us to take you to be our son. We gladly said yes. God sent you to us, which makes you extra special. We could not love you any more than what we do."

"There is a scripture that says, 'Before you were formed in your mother's womb, I knew you.' Levi, we want this beautiful story of how your life began to show you how awesome God is. It should remind you that when He created you, He knew that you were our son. This is why you look just like your dad. Because he is your dad! This is why we share so many things in common and most importantly why we all love each other so much. We could not imagine our lives without you. You are our firstborn son."

"I named you before I ever saw you. We have an
unbreakable bond."

"As time goes on, you may have questions. We are
always here to answer any questions you have, it
doesn't matter what it is. The rest of your family is
always available as well. We prayed for you and what
our lives would be like. I dreamed about you and
spoke to you although you weren't in my belly. I even
went to doctor's appointments to see how things were
going. Well, Levi, what questions do you have?"

Levi looked at us and said, "Do you know what high school Allen Iverson graduated from?"
We said, "No."
Levi proceeded to tell us more than we wanted to know about his newfound favorite player. Levi had no questions, but we told him where he came from. Levi made no big deal about the conversation. We were more nervous than he was. We told him we loved him and were here when he had questions. Levi said, "I love you too," and went back to watching Allen Iverson's highlights on YouTube.
I asked my husband, "Why do you think he reacted like that?"
He said, "Because of all the love he feels, he is secure in who he is and who we are to him. All praise to God that he has blessed us to provide a solid foundation of love, support, and security."
We had decided we would get tickets to a Houston Rockets game to celebrate that monumental conversation. We could not wait to surprise him.
Things seemed to progress as normal. There were some longer hugs and some acts to get a little more attention, but this was not concerning and not extremely out of the ordinary.

The week finally came. It was game time. We prepared for the day and acted unassumingly. The boys had no clue they were headed to the airport for not only a Houston Rockets game but their first airplane ride. This was a big deal! Our second son, Tobias, had all the questions, as usual.

"Where are we going?" he asked when he saw the luggage.

"No worries, Tobias, you will see."

We had to play it cool because if they sensed any trepidation and anxiousness, it could take a turn. We arrived at the airport and unloaded our things. Then we entered the terminal. After finally arriving at the gate, we told them, "We're taking a trip to celebrate our family! It's going to be fun."

The boys enjoyed the airplane trip; they were amazed.
The take-off was a bit tricky, but we all made it. We
stayed in a great hotel. Levi loved to swim, so we made
sure he had an opportunity to do so.
We could have just turned back around after the hotel
stay, but when we went to the arena, Levi realized
where we were and what was happening. He could not
contain himself. He screamed and jumped and went
completely crazy!
The game was great. We had so much fun. It felt like
a dream. It was all worth it, just to show Levi how
much his family loves him and how much God loves us.

Being adopted makes you super special and loved. Never doubt it, never feel out of place. If for some reason you ever do, think about your life. Think about the extra care God took to make your life. The love you have always felt and how special you must be for God to have taken such steps to get you where you belong.